science QUEST

NATIONAL GEOGRAPHIC   Washington D.C.

Digital Revolution

The Quest to Build Tiny Transistors

Glen Phelan

The concept of laptop computers came in the 1970s, but the first laptops were not as portable as they are now. Today, most laptops are small, lightweight, and very convenient.

CONTENTS

William Shockley (left), Walter Brattain (center), and John Bardeen were known as "The Dream Team" for thier invention of the transistor.

INTRODUCTION

On December 16, 1947, two scientists huddled over a strange-looking device in a research lab. They passed a weak electric signal through it, and something wonderful happened. The signal coming out was much stronger than the signal going in. The men had invented a transistor. It was the day the future began.

A family gathers around a radio to listen to their favorite programs in the 1940s.

1820

A French physicist named Andre Marie Ampere discovers how electrical currents work.

Transistors are part of every electronic device you use—from cell phones to computers. Did only two people invent the transistor? No. The work of many people led to the discovery. The story of the transistor is an inspiring tale. It's full of brilliant insight, happy accidents, and hard work. But it is also the story of fierce competition and clashing egos.

In a very short period of time, the transistor has changed our lives. To understand the effects it's had on our world, we need to go back to the 1940s—before the computer age began.

Life in the 1940s

In the first half of the 1940s, the United States was at war. Every evening, families gathered around their radios to hear the latest news about World War II battles far away. Television had been invented, but few people had them; the main sources of news were still radios and newspapers.

1863

President Abraham Lincoln instates the first national Thanksgiving Day.

A telephone from the 1940s.

While soldiers were off fighting in Europe, people at home pitched in to help the war effort. Scientists pitched in, too. They put aside their normal research and worked on projects that helped win the war. Then, in 1945, the war ended. Soldiers were coming home, and everyone looked forward to a better way of life. They wanted to buy things. They wanted new cars, new homes, and new washing machines.

The pace of life picked up, but compared to today, it was slow. There were no portable radios or CD players. And if you wanted to copy a school report, you used a copy machine, right? Wrong. They hadn't been invented yet. Instead, you put carbon paper between the pages of your report and put all the paper in your typewriter.

Where were computers? There were a few. They had already come a long way, but they didn't look like today's machines. The transistor would change all that.

> Soldiers were coming home, and everyone looked forward to a better way of life.

This counting device is called an abacus, but it was not like the calculators we use today. The abacus was used to keep track of numbers as a person did math in their head.

THE FIRST COMPUTERS

Computers were not always the electronic wonders we know today. In fact, there was a time when they weren't even electronic. The first computers were around long before electricity was even discovered.

Frenchman Blaise Pascal at age 19. Besides being an inventor, Blaise was also a mathematician and physicist.

1868

The first bicycle race on record takes place in Paris, France.

1871

P.T. Barnum's Circus, "The Greatest Show on Earth," premieres in Brooklyn, NY.

Computing by Hand

The first computer was the abacus. It was invented more than 4,000 years ago in the Middle East, and it's still used today. The abacus didn't have a screen, or a mouse, or even buttons to push. But it is a computer. That's because it helped people compute, or solve, math problems. By moving sliding beads on a rack, the user could do arithmetic to keep track of items bought or sold.

The next big breakthrough in the computing machine came centuries later. In 1642, a young Frenchman named Blaise Pascal, invented a calculator. It was a box of gears and dials that could add sums up to ten million. But, Pascal's calculator could only add.

Over the years, other people made calculators that could add, subtract, multiply, and divide. These machines were all operated by turning wheels, dials, and gears by hand.

The calculator invented by Blaise Pascal became known as the Pascaline. It used cogged wheels to perform calculations.

A Steam Computer

In the early 1800s, steam engines changed the way many things worked. Steam became an important source of power for trains, ships, and machines in cotton mills. In the 1820s, an English math professor named Charles Babbage had an idea. Why not use steam to power a computing machine?

Charles Babbage was inspired by the Jacquard loom. It used punch cards to guide the weaving pattern of cloth.

1872 Feminists, including Susan B. Anthony, are arrested for trying to vote in the presidential election.

Babbage designed a steam-powered computer. It had more than 50,000 parts. What was special about his design, however, was that this computer used punched cards. A pattern of holes was punched into each card. This pattern would tell the computer what to do. This idea gave birth to computer languages and computer programmers.

Unfortunately, Babbage never finished building his computer. One reason was that the parts could not be made precisely enough. But he did provide an important idea for others to build on. By using patterns on punched cards, he showed that it was possible to create a code to tell computers what to do.

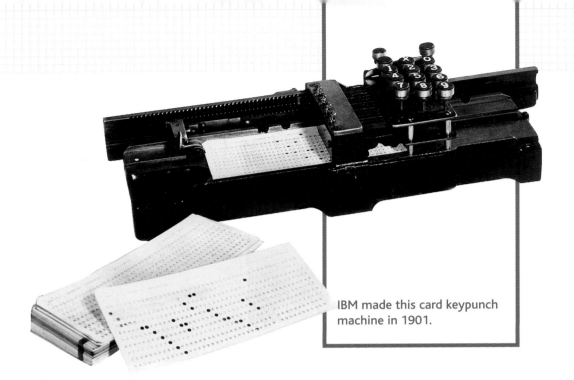

IBM made this card keypunch machine in 1901.

Counting Faster

In the 1880s, inventor Herman Hollerith had a problem. He wanted to speed up the computing of the United States census. The census is a count of the population that is made every ten years. But in 1880, the census took almost seven years to compute. With the growing population, the next census might take ten years. A faster way was needed. Hollerith invented a machine that read punched cards. The cards stored census data. Each punch on a card stood for a number. Combinations of two punches stood for letters. With the punch-card reader, a rough count of the 1890 census took only six weeks to compute!

These early computers did not run on electricity. But soon people would learn how to control the flow of electricity. That would lead to the world of electronics. It all began with the invention of a special kind of tube and an energetic inventor from Iowa.

science BOOSTER

Fun Fact
Hollerith used his punch-card reader in the business world. He founded the Tabulating Machine Company. This grew to be the giant company now known as International Business Machines, or IBM.

Lee De Forest holds his most famous invention, the vacuum tube.

A BREAKTHROUGH IN SOUND

Lee De Forest's life was filled with more failures than successes. Like many inventors, he tried lots of new and sometimes crazy things before he made his first important discovery. But Lee De Forest's invention opened the door to the world of electronics and computers. His vacuum tube made it all possible.

Lee De Forest

BORN August 25, 1873 Council Bluffs, Iowa

DIED June 30, 1961 Hollywood, California

Lee De Forest was curious as a child. He was interested in science and began inventing mechanical gadgets when he was just 13 years old.

Lee went on to study at Yale University. At Yale, his inquisitive nature drove him to tap into the school's electrical system, and he caused a campus-wide blackout. He earned a bachelor's of science degree in 1893 and a Ph.D. in 1899.

Lee is best known for his invention of the vacuum tube. Vacuum tubes were the amplifiers and switches in radios, telephones, radar, televisions, and computers until the transistor was invented.

During the 1920s, he worked on a sound system for motion pictures. Later, he turned his attention to the emerging technology of television.

1873 Lee De Forest is born.

1898 The Treaty of Paris ends the Spanish-American War.

A Drive to Invent

As a boy in the 1880s, Lee De Forest was bright, energetic, and creative. He was also ambitious. In school, he was always inventing things to sell or enter in contests. He wanted to make money to help pay for his education. He was also hoping to become rich and famous. None of his early inventions were very successful. But that didn't discourage him.

When De Forest went to college in the 1890s, he became very interested in radio. But radio as we know it hadn't been invented yet. Scientists were just beginning to try to send radio waves through the air using what was called "wireless telegraphy." After college, De Forest continued to study radio waves, and he earned an advanced degree based on his study.

1902

Walter Brattain is born.

1903

The first World Series is played.

1906

Grace Murray Hopper is born.

The vacuum tube is invented.

The First Amplifier

Then, in 1906, De Forest was tinkering with some wireless telegraph equipment. He used a light bulb with a metal plate inside it. This experiment had been conducted years before by Thomas Edison. But De Forest then put a squiggly piece of wire called a grid inside the bulb. He found that the grid acted like a switch that could turn electricity on or off. This was important.

The big breakthrough came when De Forest fed a weak electric signal into the bulb. The grid made that signal stronger. De Forest was astonished! The bulb had become an amplifier. He knew that he had invented something really useful at last. This invention made it possible to amplify, or boost, and send sound waves. Now voices and music could be sent through the air. Radio, television, and the computer were soon to follow.

> This invention made it possible to amplify, or boost, and send sound waves.

Opera singer Enrico Caruso singing in Brooklyn, New York. His singing was heard from miles away, thanks to De Forest's invention of the amplifier.

1908

John Bardeen is born.

1910

William Shockley is born.

The Sound of Music

De Forest was very excited about this new invention. He wanted to show the world what he had done. So he arranged to do the first live broadcast from the opera house in New York City. He planned to broadcast the famous opera singer Enrico Caruso.

First he set up a strange-looking transmitter in the attic of the opera house. Then he needed an antenna high enough to send signals. He ended up tying two long fishing poles to the flagpole on the roof. He was ready to broadcast.

On January 13, 1910, hundreds of people waited at listening posts around New York City. They all were wired to earphones. When the singing began, they heard the voice of Caruso in their earphones. Music had traveled for miles through the air!

Vacuum tubes switched electricity on and off. They also generated a lot of heat, which made them a lot like light bulbs.

Boosting Phone Calls

De Forest's invention came to be called the vacuum tube. It looked a lot like a light bulb, but it made electric signals stronger. In 1912, he showed it to the American Telephone and Telegraph (AT&T) company. This was just what the phone company needed. Until now, a call from New York could only go as far as Denver. It needed a boost to get all the way to the Pacific Coast. The amplifier would boost its signals. With vacuum tubes, calls could go from coast to coast.

In July 1914, the president of AT&T made the first call from coast to coast: He phoned from New York to San Francisco. The signal was boosted along the way by vacuum tubes. The boosters were in Pennsylvania, Nebraska, and Utah. The vacuum tube was a success. Soon, phone lines linked all parts of the nation, and the telephone became a common item in most homes.

Rufus P. Turner was the first African American to operate a radio broadcast station.

Radio Comes of Age

The vacuum tube paved the way for the Golden Age of Radio. The first regularly scheduled radio broadcasts came from Pittsburgh in 1920. Within a few years, radio stations sprang up across the country. By 1929, more than 10 million families owned radios.

Radio changed communication and entertainment. Now people could get the latest news and sports without waiting for the newspaper. They could tune in to hear their favorite music, comedies, and dramas. All this was possible because of vacuum tubes.

De Forest's desire for fame often led him to exaggerate.

1914

Vacuum tubes boost phone calls.

This is what a radio station looked like in the 1920s.

He even called himself the Father of Radio. But the radio was the work of many people over many years. De Forest helped, but he was not alone.

A Life of Ups and Downs

Sometimes it seemed Lee De Forest spent as much time in court as in the lab. He was involved in many lawsuits. One lawsuit contested who had made an improvement to the vacuum tube. De Forest won that one. But another time, a scientist accused De Forest of stealing an idea, and De Forest lost.

De Forest also started a number of companies to try to sell his inventions. But his companies failed. Sometimes it was because he made bad business decisions. Sometimes it was because his partners were not honest. Despite his failures, De Forest's vacuum tube was a great success—and an important breakthrough. It was a big step down the road to today's electronic world. And in the 1940s, vacuum tubes became the main parts of the first electronic computers.

science BOOSTER

Did You Know?
The vacuum tube was not De Forest's only invention. In all, he held patents for hundreds of inventions. Many were not very useful. But one of these added sound to the film used to make movies. At first, this invention was ignored. But later he won an honorary Academy Award for it.

Physicist John Mauchly works on the world's first digital computer, called the electronic numerical integrator and computer, or ENIAC for short.

ENIAC: THE FIRST ELECTRONIC COMPUTER

In February 1946, right after World War II ended, the U.S. Army unveiled a secret weapon. Was it a super-accurate missile? A powerful tank? No. It was a computer. It worked because of vacuum tubes. And it made every weapon more effective.

1920

Women are granted the right to vote in the United States.

1921

The lie detector test is invented.

> In just a few seconds, the computer calculated the flight path of a bullet.

Taking Aim

During World War II, soldiers who fired large guns had to know where to aim. The same was true for bomber pilots in airplanes. To hit their targets, they had to consider many factors. For example, they had to know wind speed and direction. They had to know how high and fast the plane was flying. They had to know how heavy the bombs were.

To hit their targets, soldiers used charts called firing tables, or bombing tables. The tables included a lot of data. The people who created these tables had a very important job.

The tables were made by about 200 female mathematicians who worked at the University of Pennsylvania. These women were called "computers." They used paper, pencils, and desktop calculators to compute the data in each table. Each of their calculations took days.

1927

Bell Labs demonstrates wireless television.

1928

Penicillin is invented.

1929

The Great Depression begins.

Processing Numbers

The Army wanted to do the calculations faster. And so they hired John Mauchly and J. Presper Eckert to work on this problem. To solve the problem, the men built the world's first digital computer. They called their machine ENIAC. This is short for electronic numerical integrator and computer.

ENIAC was immense. It weighed 30 tons and filled a large room. It had 18,000 vacuum tubes and 6,000 switches. On February 14, 1946, Mauchly and Eckert showed others how ENIAC worked. People were amazed. In just a few seconds, the computer calculated the flight path of a bullet.

Operating ENIAC

But making ENIAC work wasn't as simple as pushing a button. Before ENIAC could solve a problem, the six women who worked on it had lots to do. They had to figure out how to wire vacuum tubes together. They had to decide how to adjust the switches. No software told ENIAC how to work. The women did that job. They were called computer operators. But they were really the first modern computer programmers.

science BOOSTER

Fun Fact
ENIAC did not always do what people wanted it to do. When the machine wouldn't work, the inventors called it MANIAC.

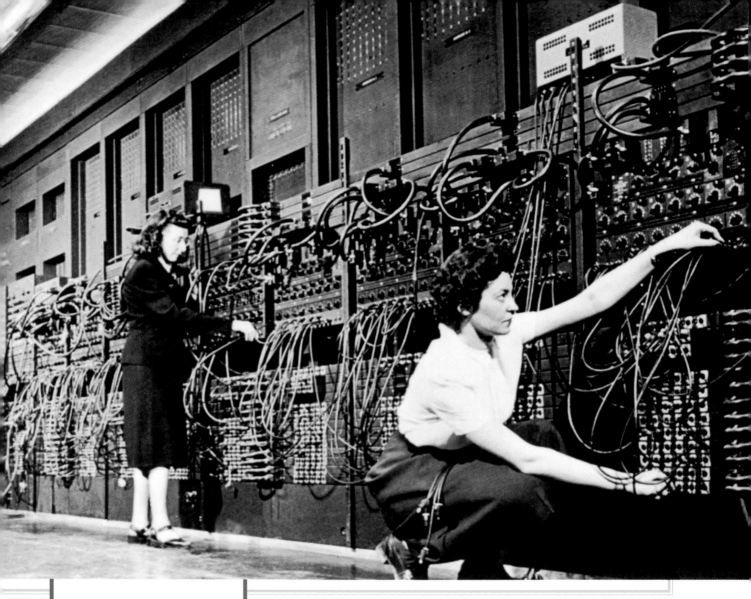

It took six computer operators to wire vacuum tubes together before ENIAC, the first digital computer, could make calculations.

Computers had come a long way since the abacus. Now they were powered by electricity and performed more complicated tasks. But they still had a long way to go to become the helpful tools they are today.

The Trouble with Tubes

ENIAC worked because of vacuum tubes. But vacuum tubes were not trouble-free. The first problem was that they were big. Even small ones were the size of light

1939–1945

World War II

1946

ENIAC computes
with vacuum tubes.

bulbs. Any machine with vacuum tubes had to be large. That's why ENIAC took up a whole room and why early radios were as big as a dresser.

Vacuum tubes also used a lot of power. ENIAC used enough electricity to power a small town. And vacuum tubes gave off a lot of heat. Large computers needed huge cooling systems to keep them cool enough to work right. And vacuum tubes, like light bulbs, burned out and had to be replaced. For ENIAC, bushel baskets of extra tubes were kept on hand. Many people were kept busy just replacing the tubes.

For computers to become more useful, someone had to invent a substitute for the vacuum tube. A team was already working on the problem—and the future was about to begin.

This view is from atop the Bell Labs headqurters in New York City in 1945. Shockley, Bardeen, and Brattain worked nearby at the Bell Labs Plant in Murray Hill, New Jersey.

THE DREAM TEAM 4

Life was busy after World War II. Soldiers returning home were marrying and settling down. People wanted new products of all kinds. Research was leading the way, and Bell Labs was a center of invention. One special team there was about to make a huge breakthrough.

1947 Transistors are invented.

Operators once had to plug each telephone call into a switchboard to make a connection.

Replacing Tubes

In the 1940s, AT&T was the main long-distance phone company in the United States, and business was good. In fact, business was almost too good. For every long-distance call, an operator had to plug in wires to make a connection. As the number of calls grew, AT&T found it hard to keep up.

The phone company needed a way to route calls automatically and more quickly. Vacuum tubes were used as amplifiers and switches. But the problems of size, heat, and burning out made them unreliable. There had to be a better way!

Bell Labs Tackles the Problem

Bell Labs was the research center for AT&T. The director of the lab had an idea. He thought that certain solid materials might act like vacuum tubes. He knew he needed a material that wouldn't get hot, burn out, break, or take up a lot of space.

1949

Russia tests the first atomic bomb.

To replace the vacuum tubes, Bell Labs put together a team of about 25 people. The team included scientists, engineers, and technicians. At the center of the team were three brilliant men.

William Shockley was the leader of the team. He had worked for Bell Labs before the war. In fact, he and another member of the team, William Brattain, had already tried and failed to find a replacement for the vacuum tube. Now they were working again on the same problem.

Building the Team

Shockley then hired John Bardeen to join the team. This was a great choice. Brattain and Bardeen worked very well together, and Shockley was their leader. They each brought a special talent to the team. Brattain could build or fix almost anything. He put the experiments together. Bardeen and Shockley offered ideas that helped direct and explain the experiments.

science BIOGRAPHY

William Shockley

BORN **February 13, 1910**
London, England

DIED **August 12, 1989**
Palo Alto, California

William Shockley's interest in science was sparked by a neighbor who taught physics at nearby Stanford University. After receiving a Ph.D. from M.I.T., William joined Bell Labs in 1936.

When World War II began, William was recruited by the military, where he helped change the way the Navy searched for submarines. He also helped train Army bomber crews and eventually won a National Medal of Merit for his work.

In 1956, he shared the Nobel Prize for Physics with Brattain and Bardeen for inventing the transistor.

Later, he started Shockley Semiconductor in Northern California, the first company in what today is known as Silicon Valley.

Walter Brattain

BORN **February 10, 1902**
Amoy, China

DIED **October 13, 1987**
Seattle, Washington

Walter Brattain spent his childhood being a cowboy and helping out on his family's cattle ranch. At school, he enjoyed math and physics, and continued to study those subjects in college.

Walter began his career as a radio engineer but was soon after offered a job at Bell Labs, working on the development of amplifiers. He worked closely with John Bardeen, and the two shared what was known as the "Miracle Month." They had one great idea after another for four straight weeks.

In 1956, Walter shared the Nobel Prize for Physics with John Bardeen and William Shockley for inventing the transistor. Later, Walter taught physics at Whitman College in Washington State, where he listened to music being played on transistors he had helped create.

1950

The Peanuts comic strip premiers with Snoopy, Charlie Brown, and the gang.

Even though the men worked well together, they had differences that later led to trouble. Shockley was very competitive. He liked to take charge. Bardeen was quiet and shy. Brattain and Bardeen were not interested in publicity, but Shockley was. None of this mattered while they worked on their experiments. But it would later break apart this great team.

The Team's First Try

It was 1945, and Shockley knew what Bell Labs wanted. He thought he knew how to make a solid-state amplifier. It would not use a vacuum tube. Instead, it would be made out of a solid material. For the material, Shockley chose silicon. He knew it could be made to conduct electric current.

Shockley tested his idea. It didn't work. There was no increase of electricity through his device. Shockley asked Bardeen to check his calculations. They were correct. The idea should have worked, but it didn't. Shockley then assigned Bardeen and Brattain to find out why.

1951
The first videotape recorder
(VTR) is invented.

1952
The summer Olympics are held
in Helsinki, Finland.

John Bardeen

BORN **May 23, 1908**
Madison, Wisconsin

DIED **January 30, 1991**
Boston, Massachusetts

John Bardeen showed such
intelligence as a child that
his parents moved him from
third grade to junior high.
Despite his mother's death
when he was 12, John man-
aged to work hard and
entered the University
of Wisconsin at age 15.

Bardeen taught at the
University of Minnesota
and then worked for the
U.S. Navy during World War
II. He helped develop ways
to protect U.S. ships against
attacks. After the war, he
joined Bell Labs.

Bardeen won two Nobel
Prizes for physics. He shared
the 1956 prize with William
Shockley and Walter Brattain
for inventing the transistor.
In 1972, he shared the prize
for developing the theory of
superconductivity, the ability
to conduct electricity without resistance.

For two years, Bardeen and Brattain experimented. The
device still would not work. But teamwork kept spirits
high. The whole team met often. Ideas flowed freely.
One idea led to another.

Water to the Rescue

In the winter of 1947, progress came quickly. It was partly
by accident. Water got on a piece of silicon used in an
experiment. When Brattain ran the experiment, he was
surprised. He found that electricity was being amplified.
This device did the same thing the vacuum tube did—
but how? The water must have increased the flow of
electrons. The team knew it was onto something.

Over the next few weeks, Bardeen and Brattain refined
their tests. They used different materials. They moved
them around. They ended up with a strange-looking
gadget. Yet it worked beautifully. A weak signal entered
the device. When the signal came out, it was much
stronger. The solid-state amplifier was born!

Sir Edmund Hillary and Tenzing Norgay climb Mt. Everest.

John Bardeen (left), William Shockley(center), and Walter Brattain at Bell Labs in the late 1940s.

Pride and Jealousy

Shockley was proud of Bardeen and Brattain's success. But he was disappointed, too. He had been part of the invention, but he hadn't been there when it happened. He wasn't as involved as he would have liked. Shockley was jealous.

But Shockley also had great insight and could tell how useful an invention might be. It was clear that the new amplifier could do what vacuum tubes had done. However, Shockley could see that in this form it would not be very useful. So he started to improve it. He didn't tell the team. When Bardeen and Brattain found out, they were stunned.

Then, Bell Labs wanted to take a publicity photo. The picture was supposed to show the birth of the new device. Shockley sat in Brattain's place. He was surrounded by equipment. The photo made it look as if Shockley was most involved in the invention. Yet he hadn't even been part of Bardeen's and Brattain's experiments.

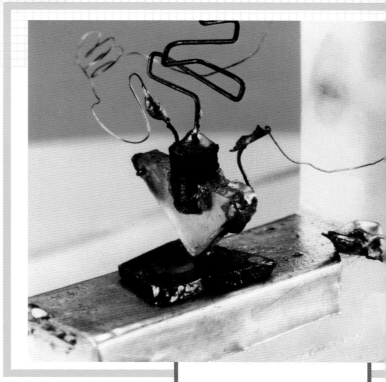

The first transistor was built by Walter Brattain. It was about half an inch tall.

Finding a Name

By 1948, the amplifier had been improved and made smaller. Now the device was ready to be made public. Only one problem remained—what to call it. Bell Labs wanted a catchy name, something people could pronounce and remember. Many names were suggested, but nothing seemed right.

An engineer who also wrote science-fiction stories came up with a solution. The engineer combined the names of similar devices. He combined the name resistor with the idea that electrons are being transferred through the new device. Trans-resistor became transistor.

Finally, on June 30, 1948, the transistor was announced to the world. Now it was time to put this little wonder to work. Over the next few years, the transistor gave birth to even smaller and more powerful offspring.

A worker assembles tiny transistors under a magnifying glass in 1954.

A NEW ERA

5

Bell Labs had its replacement for the vacuum tube. The transistor not only improved phone service—it also changed lives, especially the lives of young people. And it would soon create a whole new computer industry.

1954

The first transistor radios are sold.

1958

The integrated circuit (microchip) is invented.

1959

Fidel Castro becomes dictator of Cuba.

> As the price of transistor radios was dropping, rock-and-roll was taking off.

Music to Go

Other companies soon joined Bell Labs in making transistors. The military had many uses for them. The device was also used in hearing aids. But for the general public, the main use for transistors was in radios.

The first transistor radios came out in 1954. Expensive for that time, they cost $50, and they sold like hot cakes. Imagine how amazing they were! The radio had been a piece of living-room furniture. Now it could fit in a pocket. People could take music with them wherever they went.

As the price of transistor radios was dropping, rock-and-roll was taking off. For the first time, kids could listen to music out of earshot of their parents. Teens could listen to Elvis Presley and Chuck Berry at the beach, in the park, or walking down the street. Parents might prefer Big Band swing, but teens were dancing to a brand-new beat.

Rock-and-roll star Elvis Presley was one of the most popular singers of the 1950s, and with the invention of the transistor radio, his fans could listen to his music wherever they wanted.

From Radios to Computers

The transistor radio became the first important instrument of the information age. People in the middle of nowhere with no electric lines could get the latest news from battery-operated transistor radios. More ideas flowed from culture to culture.

The transistors used in the 1950s and 1960s were based on the new design that Shockley had created without telling Bardeen and Brattain. He had known the transistor made by Bardeen and Brattain would be hard to produce. It would break too easily. He redesigned it to solve these problems. The phone company was still using Bardeen and Brattain's device. But it was Shockley's device that appeared in transistor radios.

Grace Murray Hopper

BORN December 9, 1906
New York, New York

DIED January 1, 1992
Alexandria, Virginia

Grace Murray Hopper graduated from Vassar College and became the first woman to receive a Ph.D. in mathematics from Yale University. She loved math and spent the early part of her career as a teacher.

Grace joined the U.S. Naval Reserve in 1943, where she worked as the first programmer for the Mark I calculator. She invented COBOL, one of the first computer languages, and also helped design a computer known as UNIVAC.

Hopper retired from the Navy in 1986 as a rear admiral and was the oldest officer in the Navy. In her honor, USS *Hopper* was launched in 1996, becoming just the second U.S. Navy warship to be named for a woman.

1967
The first calculators with microchips are invented.

1964
The Beatles perform on *The Ed Sullivan Show*.

The transistor also started a new generation of computers when it replaced the vacuum tube. Even though transistors still had to be connected with wires, they took up a lot less space. As a result, computers became smaller and more dependable. They did their work faster, too. But they were expensive. Only a few businesses, universities, and government agencies could afford them.

New Languages

Progress came quickly in making computers into useful tools for ordinary people. Part of that progress came with the development of computer languages. A computer language is a set of instructions that tells the computer how to work. Different languages have different purposes. Some are for word processing. Some are for business uses. Some are for making art.

Grace Murray Hopper invented one of the first user-
friendly computer languages. Often called "Amazing Grace,"
Hopper was always looking for better ways to do things.
In 1959, she invented COBOL (Common Business-Oriented
Language). It allowed a user to type English words, instead
of numbers and symbols, to tell the computer what to do.
Such user-friendly languages meant a person could use a
computer without being an expert.

Silicon Valley

Have you heard of Silicon Valley? That's the nickname
of the area just south of San Francisco. It's where many
computer companies established their headquarters. And
it's where Bill Shockley took his knowledge of transistors
to seek his fortune.

science BOOSTER

Fun Fact
Did you ever wonder why a
computer problem is called
a bug? In 1945, Grace Hopper
was working on a computer
that broke down. When
people looked inside the
computer, they saw a moth
caught in some wires. This
was the first computer "bug."

1968

Martin Luther King, Jr., is assassinated.

The first integrated circuit (microchip) put several transistors on a silicon plate—and started the electronic revolution.

In 1955, Shockley left Bell Labs. He headed to Palo Alto, California, where he had spent part of his childhood. He started his own company to produce transistors. He hired some of the best scientists and engineers in the country. But Shockley was not an easy man to work for. He seemed interested only in ideas that were his own. Soon, some of his best workers left to start their own transistor company.

Transistors Join Forces

Shockley's former workers started a company called Fairchild Semiconductor. They found a way to place more than one transistor on a piece of silicon. This was the first integrated circuit. It got rid of any wires between transistors. Like the transistor, the first integrated circuit was a clumsy, messy gadget. But workers soon improved it. New methods let them put more and more transistors on a circuit. Soon the integrated circuit was called a microchip, or chip. The more transistors and other parts there are on the chip, the faster the chip can work. This is because electrons travel shorter distances between parts.

This microchip is sitting on an ant's back. In the future, microchips will fit across the width of a human hair.

In the 1970s, more and more people started their own high-tech companies. They kept improving chips. Computers got smaller, cheaper, faster, and more dependable. Today, a chip can be smaller than an ant. Yet that chip all by itself is more powerful than ENIAC. And ENIAC was a big deal just 50 years ago.

Microchips make it possible for air traffic controllers to handle many flights at one time.

TODAY'S TECHNOLOGY AND BEYOND

Look around you. Do you see a transistor? A microchip? Probably not. But transistor technology is everywhere. It keeps your world running.

A circuit board on the inside of a computer is also known as the motherboard. It is where a computer houses its major components like memory and disk drives.

The Key to Computers

Nowadays, almost anything with a plug or a battery works on microchips. Each chip is like a minicomputer. It has thousands or millions of transistors. And transistors are what make all kinds of computers run.

You've probably used a computer. But even if you haven't, you use things that contain computers. Computers might be in the digital watch you're wearing. They are probably in the furnace that keeps you warm.

When you think about it, the basic things a computer does are pretty simple. Computers store, process, and retrieve information. That's it. You do the same thing when you remember something you've learned, such as a phone number or your friend's birthday.

Walter Brattain dies.

The invention of computers has made many daily tasks, like checking out at the grocery store, much faster.

Speeding Up

But there's a big difference between your information handling ability and a computer's. Computers can handle an incredible amount of information. And they do it so quickly. Computers at the grocery store can scan a bar code, translate it into a price, and add up your purchases. And they do this as fast as the clerk can pass the items over the scanner. The amazing speed of computers is why, through the Internet, you can chat with friends, order a pizza, or read a newspaper from another country.

Not all computers are small. Supercomputers can take up whole rooms, just as ENIAC did. Supercomputers analyze huge amounts of data. For example, they analyze weather data from all over the world and help scientists predict tomorrow's weather.

When you think about it, the basic things a computer does are pretty simple.

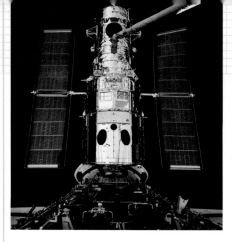

1989

William Shockley dies.

The Berlin Wall falls.

1990

The Hubble Space Telescope
is placed in orbit.

1991

John Bardeen dies.

1992

Grace Murray Hopper dies.

Possibilities at Home

Computers are part of our lives today. They could play an
even bigger role in the future. For example, chips could be
built into kitchen appliances and stereo equipment. Fiber-
optic cables could connect these objects to each other. All
the objects would connect to a main computer stored in a
closet. You could control devices from small touch screens
in every room.

Some homes of the future could be "smart." When you walk
through the door, the computer would put on your favorite
music. It would adjust the temperature just the way you
like it. Refrigerators would connect to the Internet and order
food to restock themselves. Ovens could "know" what they
are cooking. They would "learn" this from microchips in
food packages.

At School and Beyond

Many students already use computers at school. You can use the Internet for assignments. You can make class presentations using a computer screen. In the future, a large computer screen may replace the chalkboard. Already, students in different countries use the Internet to work together on projects. But in the future, this kind of long-distance collaboration could be a common part of the day. Instead of reading about other places or watching a video, you'll be able to go there—through virtual reality, that is. You might take a virtual walk on the Great Wall of China. You might climb a mountain in Peru and tour museums in Paris.

It is exciting to think how different the world of technology will be in 20 years. Just imagine the possibilities—and one day you might make them happen.

Computers are a big part of our lives at work and at school, but they also provide us with entertainment. Computers are found in many toys, and they are what make video games work.

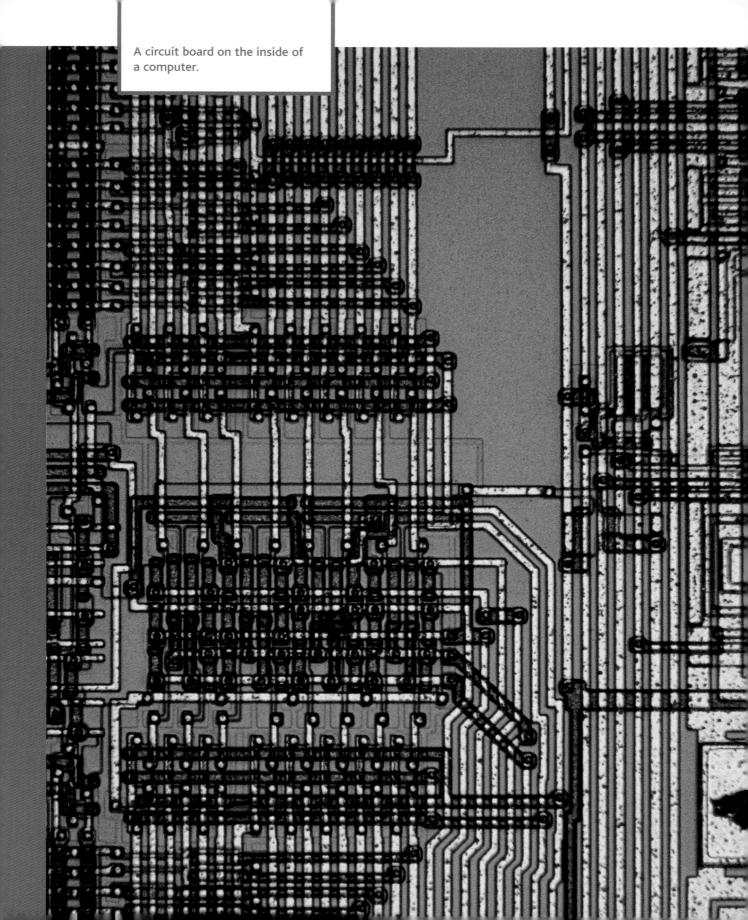

A circuit board on the inside of a computer.

Abacus
device for calculating that has beads on a rack

Amplifier
any electronic device for increasing the strength of a signal or the strength of a current

Calculator
mechanical or electronic device that performs mathematical operations

COBOL
one of the first computer languages to be written. It is used to solve problems in business.

Computer language
a set of instructions that tells a computer what to do

Digital
relating to data in numerical form. A digital computer operates with numbers. A digital watch shows the time in numbers instead of showing hands on a dial.

Electricity
a form of energy produced by the movement of electrons

Electronic
the use of electricity to carry information in the form of signals

Fiber optic
relating to thin fibers of glass or plastic that carry information in the form of light

Integrated circuit
network of transistors and the connections among them, placed on a thin piece of silicon

Microchip
another name for an integrated circuit. It is often called a chip, for short.

Patent
document that protects an inventor's rights to his or her invention

Silicon
an element occurring in the earth's crust that is used in electronic devices

Software
programs, procedures, and written instructions for a computer

Solid-state amplifier
amplifier made from a solid material instead of a vacuum tube

Transistor
device made from a solid material that can act as an electronic switch or an amplifier

Vacuum tube
device consisting of a sealed area where electrons flow between electronic conductors separated by a vacuum

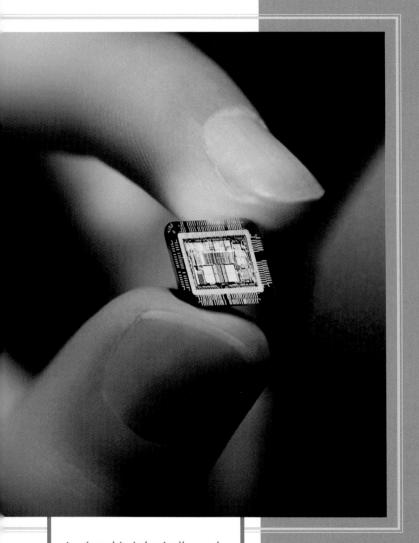

A microchip is basically made up of three parts, a silicon chip where information is transmitted, an iron core that receives signals, and an energy-storing device called a capacitor.

Biographical Resources

Want to learn more about the different radios Lee De Forest invented? Visit www.deforestradio.com to see images of his inventions and read more about his important contributions to the field of transistors.

After working with John Bardeen and William Brattain at Bell Labs, William Shockley established Shockley Semiconductor in 1955, the first company in the area known today as Silicon Valley. To get an idea of what it was like to work at Shockley Semiconductor, click on http://www.pbs.org/transistor/background1/events/shocksemi.html.

Take a peek at Walter Brattain's lab notes on the development of the amplifier. Go to http://www.pbs.org/transistor/science/labpages/labpg1.html to get an even better understanding of the work he was doing at Bell Labs.

Read more about Grace Hopper and her military career at http://www.hopper.navy.mil/grace/grace.htm, and find out why she was nicknamed "Amazing Grace."

Other Cool Science Stuff About Transistors

Want to learn more about radio waves and how they transmit sounds? Go to http://www.pbs.org/wgbh/aso/tryit/radio to understand how we're able to hear sounds and music from faraway places.

For a complete timeline of the history of computers, visit the Computer History Museum's "This Day in History" online exhibit, at www.computerhistory.org/tdih/index.php. You can search by week, or month, for all of the discoveries that have occurred over the past 50 years.

These days, computers are everywhere, even places we don't think about. To see how far we've come since the first computer was invented, go to http://www.kidputer.com/. There you'll be able to see how our lives have been affected by technology, and what might be ahead in the future.

To read more about Silicon Valley and how the area has influenced technology, go to www.siliconvalleyhistory.org.

What More Can I Do?

Learn more about the history of computers through crossword puzzles! Click on www.surfnetkids.com/games/computerhistory-cw.htm to play.

Grace Murray Hopper invented COBOL, one of the first computer languages, but computers these days are capable of handling more complex languages. HTML is the language used for communication on the World Wide Web. Go to http://www.goodellgroup.com/tutorial/, and you'll soon understand how to build your own Web pages!

Learn more fun facts about computer history and how computers work. Visit http://www.factmonster.com/ipka/A0772279.html

Also, try heading out to your local science museum or library for more information and fun facts.

RESOURCES

INDEX

Copyright © 2006
National Geographic Society

Published by the National
Geographic Society.

All rights reserved. Reproduction
of the whole or any part of the
contents without written permission
from the National Geographic
Society is strictly prohibited.

Large parts of this book were previously
published as *Building Tiny Transistors*
(National Geographic Reading
Expeditions), copyright © 2003.

Book design by KINETIK. The body
text of the book is set in Bliss Regular.
The display text is set in Filosofia.

Library of Congress Cataloging-in-
Publication Data

Phelan, Glen.
Digital revolution : the quest to build
tiny transistors / by Glen Phelan.
p. cm. — (Science quest)
Includes bibliographical references and
index.
Trade ISBN-10: 0-7922-5545-3
Trade ISBN-13: 978-0-7922-5545-1
Library ISBN-10: 0-7922-5546-1
Library ISBN-13: 978-0-7922-5546-8
1. Transistor circuits—Design and con-
struction. I. Title. II. Science quest
(National Geographic Society (U.S.)).
TK7871.92.P44 2006
621.3815'28—dc22

2006005697

PUBLISHED BY THE
NATIONAL GEOGRAPHIC SOCIETY

John M. Fahey, Jr.,
President and Chief Executive Officer

Gilbert M. Grosvenor,
Chairman of the Board

Nina D. Hoffman,
*Executive Vice President, President of
Books & Education Publishing Group*

Ericka Markman, *Senior Vice President,
President of Children's Books & Education
Publishing Group*

Stephen Mico, *Senior Vice President &
Publisher of Children's Books and
Education Publishing Group*

Bea Jackson, *Design Director, Children's
Books & Education Publishing Group*

Margaret Sidlosky, *Illustrations Director,
Children's Books & Education Publishing
Group*

PREPARED BY NATIONAL GEOGRAPHIC
CHILDREN'S BOOKS

Nancy Laties Feresten, *Vice President,
Editor-in-Chief of Children's Books*

Jim Hiscott, *Art Director, Children's Books
& Education Publishing Group*

Susan Kehnemui Donnelly,
Priyanka Lamichhane, *Project Editors*

KINETIK, *Designer*

Lori Epstein, *Illustrations Editor*

Jean Cantu, *Illustrations Coordinator*

Debbie Guthrie Haer, *Copy Editor*

Rebecca Hinds, *Managing Editor*

R. Gary Colbert, *Production Director*

Lewis R. Bassford, *Production Manager*

Vincent P. Ryan, Maryclare Tracey,
Manufacturing Managers

PROGRAM DEVELOPMENT FOR
NATIONAL GEOGRAPHIC READING
EXPEDITIONS
Kate Boehm Jerome

CONSULTANT/REVIEWERS
Dr. James Shymansky, E. Desmond
Lee Professor of Science Education,
University of Missouri-St. Louis

Cover: Cover:© Bettmann/Corbis; 4-5:
Chris Knapton/Photo Researchers; 6: ©
Jim Craigmyle/Corbis; 8-9: Property of
AT&T Archives—reprinted with permis-
sion of AT&T; 10: © Bettmann/Corbis;
11: Petrified Collection/Getty Images;
12-13: Steve Mercer/Getty Images; 14:
SPL/Photo Researchers; 15: Jean-Loup
Charmet/Photo Researchers; 16: Bill
Ballenberg/National Museum of
American History;17: © Bettmann
/Corbis; 18-19: © Bettmann/Corbis; 20:
© Corbis; 21: © Bettmann/Corbis; 22: ©
Bettmann/Corbis; 23: Property of AT&T
Archives—reprinted with permission of
AT&T; 24: © Corbis; 25: © Bettmann
/Corbis; 26-27: © Bettmann/Corbis; 28:
© Bettmann/Corbis; 29: ©Bettmann
/Corbis; 30: LANL/Photo Researchers;
31: Jody Dole/Getty Images; 32-33: ©
Bettmann/Corbis; 34: Archive Holdings
Inc./Getty Images; 35: AP/Wide World
Photos; 36: © Bettmann /Corbis; 37:

Emilio Segré Visual Archives, Meggers
Gallery of Nobel Laureates; 38: (left):
Property of AT&T Archives—reprinted
with permission of AT&T; 38 (right): ©
John Van Hasselt/Corbis; 39: Property of
AT&T Archives—reprinted with permis-
sion of AT&T; 40-41: David Sarnoff
Library, Princeton, New Jersey; 42: Classic
PIO Partners; 43: ©Bettmann /Corbis; 44
(left): AP/Wide World Photos; 44 (right):
Courtesy of Texas Instruments; 45: ©
Bettmann /Corbis; 46: Courtesy of Texas
Instruments; 47: © Kurt Stier /Corbis; 48-
49: © Steve Liss/Corbis; 50: Tomi/
PhotoLink/Getty Images; 51: © Chuck
Savage/Corbis; 52: © NASA/Roger
Ressmeyer/Corbis; 53: ©Ausloeser/zefa
/Corbis; 54-55: E. Pollard/PhotoLink/Getty
Images; 56: Jeff Sherman/Getty Images.

One of the world's largest nonprofit scien-
tific and educational organizations, the
National Geographic Society was founded
in 1888 "for the increase and diffusion of
geographic knowledge." Fulfilling this
mission, the Society educates and inspires
millions every day through its magazines,
books, television programs, videos, maps
and atlases, research grants, the National
Geographic Bee, teacher workshops, and
innovative classroom materials. The Society
is supported through membership dues,
charitable gifts, and income from the sale
of its educational products. This support is
vital to National Geographic's mission to
increase global understanding and promote
conservation of our planet through explo-
ration, research, and education.

For more information, please call

1-800-NGS-LINE (647-5463)
or write to the following address:

NATIONAL GEOGRAPHIC SOCIETY
1145 17th Street N.W.
Washington, D.C. 20036-4688
U.S.A.

For information about special discounts for
bulk purchases, please contact National
Geographic Books Special Sales:
ngspecsales@ngs.org

Visit the Society's Web site:
www.nationalgeographic.com

Printed in Belgium.